The EXPECTED One

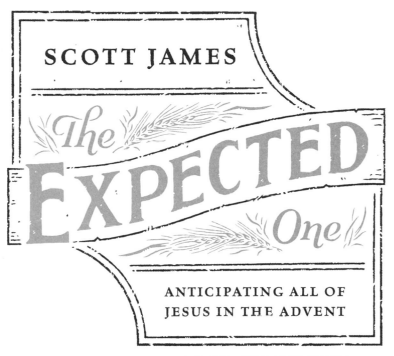

SCOTT JAMES

The
EXPECTED
One

ANTICIPATING ALL OF
JESUS IN THE ADVENT

FOREWORD BY DAVID PLATT

B&H
PUBLISHING
NASHVILLE, TENNESSEE

Published by B&H Publishing Group
Nashville, Tennessee

Dewey Decimal Classification: 242.33
Subject Heading: DEVOTIONAL LITERATURE
/ ADVENT / CHRISTMAS

Unless otherwise noted, all Scripture quotations
are taken from the Christian Standard Bible®,
Copyright © 2017 by Holman Bible Publishers.
Used by permission. Christian Standard Bible®
and CSB® are federally registered trademarks of
Holman Bible Publishers.

Cover design and illustrations
by Stephen Crotts.

1 2 3 4 5 6 7 • 25 24 23 22 21

For my son, Will.
Always look to Him—the Joy
of every longing heart.

THE ORDER
OF THINGS

FOREWORD

———

BY DAVID PLATT

When we consider the mystery and majesty of God during Christmas, we realize that the birth of His Son and our Savior did not randomly appear on the pages of human history. Instead, over a period spanning more than a thousand years, God provided hundreds of prophecies concerning the coming of Christ, and on that evening in a stable in Bethlehem, the heavens and the earth witnessed the culmination of those promises from God to His people.

In light of these prophecies, it is extremely helpful for followers of Christ to pause before Christmas and consider the promises that preceded Christ's birth. Further, it is deeply meaningful for God's people to gather together with family and/or friends in the days leading up to December 25 simply to contemplate the glory of the baby to whom all of history pointed and around whom all of history revolves. Jesus has come, Jesus has died, Jesus has risen, and Jesus will forever reign! Certainly these are themes worthy of our reflection.

For this reason, I enthusiastically recommend *The Expected One*, an Advent guide that one of the pastors at The Church at Brook Hills, Scott James, has written. It can be used in many different ways, whether alone, with your family, with friends, in a small group, or even as a church altogether. Scott faithfully serves children and their parents at Brook Hills, and he has written with a keen eye specifically aimed on fostering faith in the hearts of children. Ultimately, my prayer is that as you walk through this material (and most importantly the Scriptures referenced herein), you might feel in a fresh way the sense of anticipation that captivated God's people who waited for Christ in the past, and that you might experience in a new way the sheer exhilaration that compels God's people to worship Christ in the present. ✦

INTRODUCTION:
"HE'S COMING!"

—

This shout of anticipation is the heart of Advent, the time of year when we look forward to the birth of Jesus Christ. As we prepare our hearts during the weeks leading up to Christmas Day, we have an opportunity to reflect upon God's priceless gift to us: the child Jesus. Rejoicing in Jesus' birth certainly brings glory to God, but sometimes we can forget that God didn't just send a child into the world; He sent a mighty Rescuer!

The image of the baby in the manger should fill our hearts with praise because we know what that baby would grow up to accomplish— He would save His people from their sins. This story is not just for those of us who live *after* Jesus' time, though. The people of God have always known what Jesus' mission would be. How did they know about this divine rescue plan before Jesus actually came? Because God promised the whole plan to them, and every single part of it was designed to become true in Jesus. He truly was the *Expected One*.

No, God didn't just promise His people that a miracle child would be born. He also promised that this child would grow up to be the loving Shepherd of His people, the place-switching Sacrifice, the resurrected Lord, and the righteous King who reigns in glory forever. But there is yet another promise: this King is coming back for His people! As we celebrate the first coming of the Expected One during Advent, let's also look forward in hopeful anticipation of His second coming. Let's keep in mind the whole picture of who Jesus is, worshipping Him as the fulfillment of all of God's promises to us, "For every one of God's promises is 'Yes' in Him" (2 Cor. 1:20).

The Old Testament passages laid out here are meant to guide you through the wide range of promises God gave us regarding His Son. They are by no means comprehensive, and not every one of them was a direct prophecy of Christ. Some were simply a sign of what was to come. All of them do, however, point to Jesus, collectively unfolding the promises of His long-awaited coming, His marvelous birth, His blameless life, His agonizing death, His glorious resurrection, and His reign as the eternal King of all. In order to express these truths, the passages here are arranged into six parts to reflect the glory of these different aspects of God's promises like a multifaceted jewel.

This book is primarily designed for families with children, but my hope is that anyone wanting to meditate deeply on the coming of Christ will find it helpful. Each day has a passage of Scripture accompanied by a brief explanation to help us "Trace the Thread" of God's unfolding plan throughout the Old Testament. These devotional thoughts are intentionally concise and are designed to prompt your own time of reflection, discussion, and prayer. Each day therefore also includes a series of questions and prayer points to guide the whole family through the weeks of Advent. There are "Connect with Kids" questions to help foster thought and conversation during family worship (along with suggested answers given in parentheses to help parents guide the discussion). You'll also find an additional question to help guide people of all ages into "Further Reflection," as well as a call to prayer in the form of a "Prayer Point" that connects to the day's passage.

If you are using these devotionals with your family, consider having a set time each day when you slow down, gather together, and worship God as a family. Perhaps sing a favorite hymn or carol before diving into the day's passage and discussion. However you use your time together, it is my prayer that this Advent season will be one of rich, gospel-centered reflection for you and your family as you make much of Christ. ✦

For a free guide to help with family worship, please go to www.theexpectedonebook.com for suggested ideas.

PART ONE

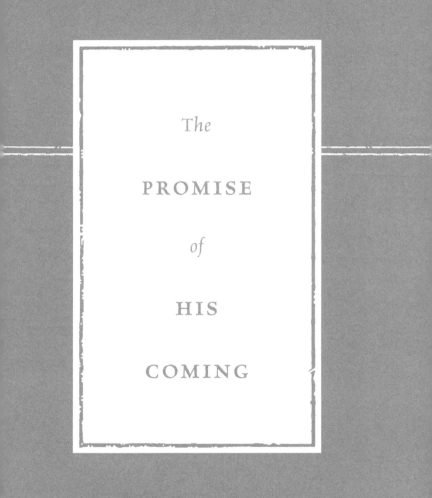

The

PROMISE

of

HIS

COMING

DECEMBER 1

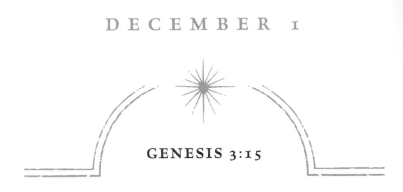

GENESIS 3:15

—

I will put hostility between you and the woman, and between your offspring and her offspring. He will strike your head, and you will strike his heel.

—

—

Although His perfect creation had just been corrupted by the arrival of sin, God promised that sin and Satan would not have the final victory. The Rescuer would come to crush Satan, ending the rebellion he led against God. His people may have been under the curse of sin, but God promised them that He would fight for them and win them back to Himself.

Hostility means that two things are against each other. What set God and Satan against each other?

Satan turned against God,
and then tempted man to do the same.

Who does this verse say will defeat Satan in the end?

The offspring of woman—this points to Jesus.

How does it make you feel knowing that God has already written the end of the story?

It gives us confidence that God is in control.

—

Christ is our great Victor, defeating an enemy that we never could. Knowing that He intercedes on our behalf (Romans 8:34), meditate on what this means to you.

PRAYER POINT

Take some time to praise God for His perfect plan to rescue us from our sin and rebellion. Tell Him how grateful you are that, in Christ, the victory is won. ✦

DECEMBER 2

ISAIAH 11:1

—

Then a shoot will grow from the stump of Jesse,
and a branch from his roots will bear fruit.

—

God chose the nation of Israel to be the people through whom the Rescuer would come. Because of their disobedience, God sometimes referred to Israel as a cut-down tree. From this stump, God promised that the Rescuer would shoot forth like a fruitful branch from the family of an Israelite named Jesse.

To what nation did Jesse belong?

The nation of Israel.

A new branch sprouting out of a tree stump is a picture of life coming from death. Can you think of any other examples of life coming from death?

Parents, talk with your children about how spring follows winter, or how a dead stalk of wheat carries the seeds for next year's harvest. Then lead your discussion to the ultimate example: Jesus Christ rose from the dead.

—

Imagine watching and waiting for a fresh shoot to grow out of an old stump. Think about the anticipation, and perhaps even the doubt, that the Israelites may have felt as they watched and waited for their Savior. How do you feel as you wait for His second coming?

———————————

PRAYER POINT

Ask God to fill your heart with hopeful anticipation as you long for His return. ✦

DECEMBER 3

JEREMIAH 23:5

—

"Look, the days are coming"—this is the LORD's declaration—"when I will raise up a Righteous Branch for David. He will reign wisely as king and administer justice and righteousness in the land."

—

King David, the son of Jesse, was Israel's greatest king. He was a man after God's own heart, but he was not a perfect king. One day, there would come another king from the line of David whose reign would be marked by perfect righteousness.

Righteousness means doing what is right and avoiding what is wrong. Who determines what is right and wrong?

God does. So, being righteous means obeying God.

Yesterday's verse spoke of a branch coming out of the stump of Jesse. David was Jesse's son; he was a good king, but he was not perfectly righteous. He still sinned. Can you think of a king from David's family who never sinned?

King Jesus.

How was it possible for Jesus to live without sinning?

Because Jesus is God.

In John 15:5 we are also called branches. We are described as being joined to the true vine, Jesus. How does it impact your daily walk to know that you are united with Jesus in this way?

PRAYER POINT

Thank God for His perfect righteousness. Thank Him that, through faith in Christ, He gives us credit for that righteousness. ✦

DECEMBER 4

EZEKIEL 34:23

—

I will establish over them one shepherd, my servant David, and he will shepherd them. He will tend them himself and will be their shepherd.

—

This righteous, coming King would watch closely over His people and protect them. Just like King David, He would be a servant of God and a great Shepherd who cared for His flock.

David was a caring shepherd. Jesus called Himself the Good Shepherd. How is Jesus our Shepherd?

He feeds, cares for, and protects His people—those who trust in Him.

How does it feel knowing that Jesus is caring for you in this way?

Parents, open up with your children about the deep comfort that comes from your relationship with Jesus.

—

Sheep cannot always see the hand of the shepherd at work. Can you think back to any instances when you did not appreciate God's leading or protection until after the fact?

PRAYER POINT

Ask God to help you grow in your dependence on Him, as a sheep looks to its shepherd. Ask Him to give you a greater awareness of the loving care He provides for you every day. ✦

ZECHARIAH 3:8–9

—

"Listen . . . I am about to bring my servant, the
Branch . . . and I will take away the iniquity of this
land in a single day."

—

God said His Servant would shoot up like a branch from among His people, but He would not come only to rule over them. He would also come to take away the penalty for their rebellion against God. He would show how great God is by rescuing His people from their sin.

Iniquity means sinfulness. How had God's people sinned against Him?

They had rebelled against His rule by disobeying Him.

How have we sinned against God?

Parents, talk with your children about specific ways we all disobey God's law. Let them know that you sin too and are in need of a great Savior.

How could all of this iniquity be taken away in a single day?

Because Jesus was punished for our sins all at once when He died on the cross.

—

The penalty for sin has already been paid, but we are not yet free from its presence. What tensions do you feel between these two truths? If God has declared you righteous in Christ, how is that truth encouraging you to grow in personal righteousness as well?

PRAYER POINT

Take some time to praise God for the astonishing fact that He sent His Son Jesus to rescue us from our sin. ✦

PART TWO

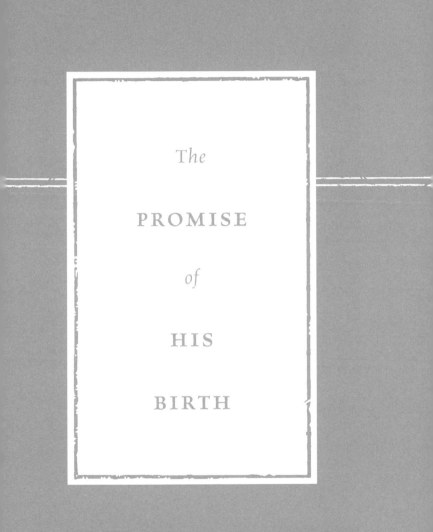

The

PROMISE

of

HIS

BIRTH

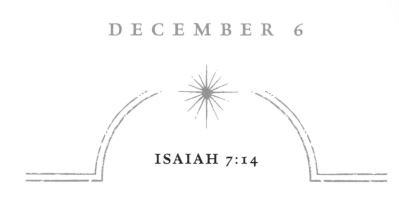

ISAIAH 7:14

—

Therefore, the Lord himself will give you a sign: See, the virgin will conceive, have a son, and name him Immanuel.

—

—

The Expected One would be born of a young woman through a miraculous birth that could only be God's doing. This miracle would be the sign that God Himself is now with us— Immanuel. God gave this promise during a time in which it didn't even look like His people would survive; but He assured them that, as always, He had a plan for them.

Who is the young woman spoken of in this
verse?

Mary, the mother of Jesus.

In this verse, God tells us that Jesus' birth would
be a miracle. Can you think of any reasons why
Jesus' birth would need to be different than all
other births?

*Parents, encourage your children to think through some
possibilities for why Jesus came to earth in a supernatural
way. For instance, it showed that He is unique; or
it showed that salvation comes only from God.*

—

This truth is likely very familiar to you, but that shouldn't make it any less astounding. What are some ways that we tend to take God's miraculous works for granted?

———————————————

PRAYER POINT

Celebrate the miraculous! Thank God for the wonderful truth that, in Christ, He came to dwell with us. ✦

DECEMBER 7

ISAIAH 9:6

—

For a child will be born for us, a son will be given to us, and the government will be on his shoulders. He will be named Wonderful Counselor, Mighty God, Eternal Father, Prince of Peace.

—

—

God would give His people His one and only
Son. And this Son? He'd be very special—
He would be the Son of man *and* the Son
of God. This means that the Rescuer would
be specially qualified to bring sinful people
back to their holy God. His nature would be
so perfect and He would do His job so well
that His name would be worthy of the same
praise that God Himself receives.

How could a small baby be called a mighty God?

*Because even when He was a small baby,
Jesus was fully God.*

How can both God and Jesus be called "God"?

*The Bible tells us that God is three persons in one—
God the Father, Jesus the Son, and the Holy Spirit.*

Why is it important to know that Jesus is both
God and man?

*Because being God is the only way He could live a
life without sin, and being a man is the only way He
could suffer and die as a punishment for our sin.*

How does the reality of the first Advent of Christ give you confidence as you await His second Advent?

PRAYER POINT

Salvation is found in Christ alone. Praise Jesus for the way He is uniquely qualified to rescue us. ✦

MICAH 5:2

—

Bethlehem Ephrathah, you are small among the clans of Judah; one will come from you to be ruler over Israel for me. His origin is from antiquity, from ancient times.

—

—

The rescuing King—the One that God had been promising to His people from the very beginning—would come from a small town called Bethlehem. This was also the hometown of King David.

In what city does this verse say the Savior would be born?

In the city of Bethlehem.

Was Bethlehem a big city?

No, it was a very small town.

Do you think it is common for famous kings to come from small, little known cities?

No, but Jesus is not like other kings.

Bethlehem was not a likely choice to become the city of kings, but the story of redemption is a story of God making unlikely choices. What does this tell us about the character of God?

PRAYER POINT

Ask God to open your eyes to the beauty of the ordinary, and to trust that He can accomplish great things through common, everyday circumstances. ✦

MALACHI 3:1

—

"See, I am going to send my messenger, and he will clear the way before me."

—

—

God promised that He would send a messenger ahead of the Rescuer in order to help God's people recognize Him. The messenger would announce His arrival. When the time actually came, the messenger would proclaim, "Look, the Lamb of God, who takes away the sin of the world!" (John 1:29).

Why do you think God sent a messenger to tell people that the Savior had come?

He wants people to be saved, so He made sure to tell them clearly that their Savior, Jesus, had arrived.

Who was this messenger?

John the Baptist.

—

Who do you know that needs to hear the good news of Jesus, the Lamb of God who takes away our sin? What is keeping you from being God's messenger to them?

_____

PRAYER POINT

Ask God to give you the heart of a messenger. Ask Him to empower you to tell His story to all who need to hear it. ✦

PART THREE

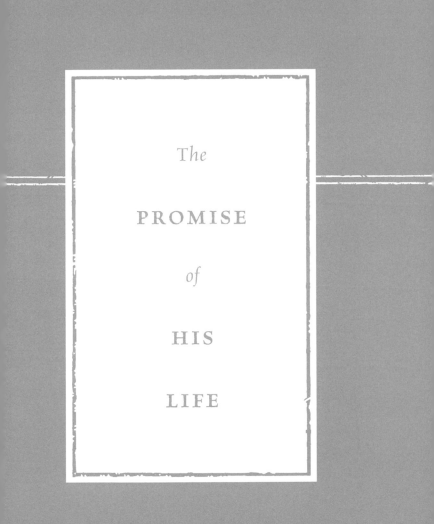

The

PROMISE

of

HIS

LIFE

ISAIAH 11:2, 5

—

The Spirit of the LORD will rest on him—a Spirit of wisdom and understanding, a Spirit of counsel and strength, a Spirit of knowledge and of the fear of the LORD. . . . Righteousness will be a belt around his hips; faithfulness will be a belt around his waist.

—

—

Unlike our lives of sin and rebellion against God, the Rescuer's life would be one of godly wisdom, righteousness, faithfulness, and respect for the Lord. Though our lives could not meet God's perfect standard, His would.

How easy is it for you to always trust in God and do what is right?

It is very hard to be completely faithful and righteous. In fact, it is impossible.

Is it good news that Jesus is completely faithful and righteous?

Yes because, by faith in Him, He gives us the credit for His faithfulness and righteousness.

By faith we are united with this righteous Lord. How should that truth affect the way we live?

PRAYER POINT

Thank God for the perfect life of Jesus Christ. Ask Him to help you trust Him and reflect His righteousness in your own life. ✦

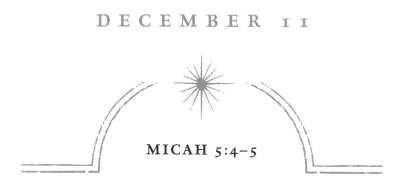

DECEMBER 11

MICAH 5:4-5

—

He will stand and shepherd them in the strength of the LORD, in the majestic name of the LORD his God. They will live securely, for then his greatness will extend to the ends of the earth. He will be their peace.

—

—

The Rescuer would be a great and mighty Shepherd to His people. In His care, the people of God would find safety and peace. Unlike other mighty men, He would not seek His own praise; He would point the people to the majesty of the One who sent Him— the Lord God.

How does a shepherd take care of his flock?

A shepherd knows his sheep, feeds them, protects them, and leads them to where they will be safe.

How does it feel to know that Jesus is your Shepherd?

Parents, talk with your children about the comfort and assurance that comes from knowing you belong to Jesus.

———

The Good Shepherd is always caring for us and holding us securely. In what ways (or particular areas of life) do you sometimes overlook these daily blessings?

———————————

PRAYER POINT

Praise Jesus for the peace and security found in Him. Ask Him to use you to help spread that peace to the ends of the earth. ✦

ZEPHANIAH 3:17

—

The LORD your God is among you, a warrior who saves. He will rejoice over you with gladness. He will be quiet in his love. He will delight in you with singing.

—

—

The Expected One wouldn't just be *sent* from God; He would *be* God. God Himself would come into this world to be among us! In His presence, true gladness and rest would be found. He would take great joy in saving His people.

Why do you think God came down to save us
Himself instead of sending someone else?

*Because God is the only One who is able
to save us. Also, it shows how important the rescue
mission is to Him—so important that He did not
mind humbling Himself to come accomplish it.*

How does saving people from sin make God
feel?

*It makes Him extremely happy,
so much that He sings with joy.*

—

What does this verse reveal about the nature of God?

PRAYER POINT

Return joy for joy. Praise the name of the Lord who delights to save. ✦

DECEMBER 13

ZECHARIAH 9:9

—

Rejoice greatly, Daughter Zion! Shout in triumph, Daughter Jerusalem! Look, your King is coming to you; he is righteous and victorious, humble and riding on a donkey, on a colt, the foal of a donkey.

—

—

The coming King would be able to save His people because of His perfect righteousness. Unlike most kings of the world, this mighty King would not come into His city in a rich processional but would humble Himself for the sake of His people. As He entered Jerusalem on a donkey, shouts of joy would be heard from the mouths of those He was coming to save.

What does it mean to be humble?

It means not thinking highly of yourself; the Bible says that humility is considering others more significant than yourself; see Philippians 2:3.

Do we normally think of important and powerful people as being proud or as being humble?

Greatness often makes people proud, but Jesus humbled Himself in order to glorify His Father and meet our greatest need.

—

Are there any recent instances in your life where you avoided following Jesus' example of humility? What distracted you from following Him in that situation?

_____

PRAYER POINT

Ask God to shape your heart to be like His and to help you grow in humility. ✦

ISAIAH 53:2-4

He grew up before him like a young plant and like a root out of dry ground. He didn't have an impressive form or majesty that we should look at him, no appearance that we should desire him. He was despised and rejected by men, a man of suffering who knew what sickness was. He was like someone people turned away from; he was despised, and we didn't value him. Yet he himself bore our sicknesses, and he carried our pains; but we in turn regarded him stricken, struck down by God, and afflicted.

—

The Rescuer would not be the kind of savior we would pick if given the chance. Most of the world, including many of His own countrymen, would reject Him because they could not believe that salvation would come from someone so plain. Even so, He would carry our pain all the way to the cross.

Did Jesus have an easy, comfortable life?

No, His life was lowly and hard. Most of the people who knew Him turned their backs on Him.

If you were in trouble and could pick someone to rescue you, do you think you would choose someone who looked weak and unimportant?

We might prefer to pick someone whose life looks powerful and highly respected, but God doesn't see things the way we do.

Even though He was despised and rejected, Jesus died for us. Why would He do that?

Because He loves us; see Romans 5:8.

—

What might have motivated God to send His Son as a common man, rather than a powerful earthly ruler?

———————

PRAYER POINT

Spend some time meditating on the fact that Jesus came as one who was despised and rejected by men. Ask God to give you a heart for the lowly and the outcast. ✦

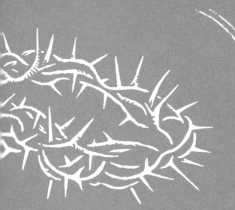

PART FOUR

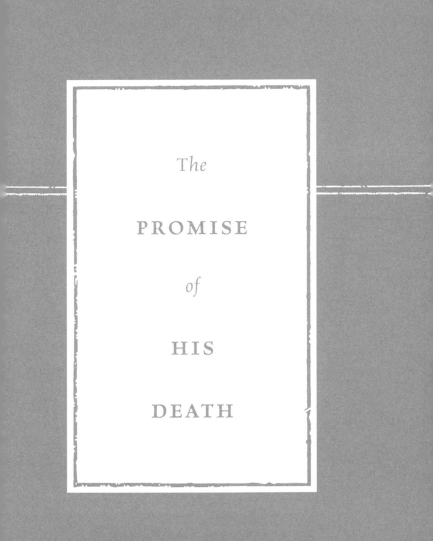

The

PROMISE

of

HIS

DEATH

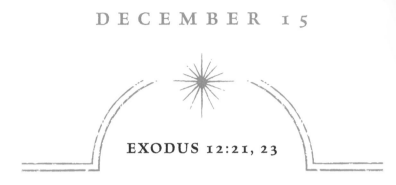

EXODUS 12:21, 23

—

Then Moses summoned all the elders of Israel and said to them, "Go, select an animal from the flock according to your families, and slaughter the Passover animal. . . . When the LORD passes through to strike Egypt and sees the blood on the lintel and the two doorposts, he will pass over the door and not let the destroyer enter your houses to strike you."

—

—

The heart of God's rescue plan would be His willingness to step in to redeem His people from judgment. Just as the Passover lamb died in order to save the lives of Israel's firstborn sons, the Rescuer would die to save His people from the curse of death.

Why did the firstborn sons of the Israelites not
die during this plague?

> *The people trusted God, who said that He would save*
> *them, and the lamb died in place of the sons.*

What did the lamb do to deserve to die?

> *Nothing, just like Jesus, who died in our place.*

With the sacrifice of an animal, the people of God had a visible reminder of the penalty for sin. Do you think this helped them grasp the serious nature of their sin? The next time you take part in the Lord's Supper, reflect on how the bread and wine serve to remind us of Jesus' sacrifice.

PRAYER POINT

Ask God to help you always remember the deadly consequences of sin. Praise Jesus for being the spotless Lamb who provides a way of salvation. ✦

LEVITICUS 16:15–16

—

"When he slaughters the male goat for the people's sin offering. . . . He will make atonement for the most holy place in this way for all their sins because of the Israelites' impurities and rebellious acts."

—

—

The punishment for sin is death. Long before the Rescuer would come, God set up a yearly sacrifice that took the punishment in place of His people. When the Rescuer arrived, He would provide the final sacrifice—once and for all.

What is a sacrifice?

A sacrifice is when something dies in order to pay the penalty for sin and to take away God's anger toward sinners.

Why did God's people have to sacrifice animals year after year?

Because the death of an animal was not enough to pay sin's penalty forever.

Why did Jesus' sacrifice only have to happen once?

Because Jesus is God. This means His sacrifice was worth so much that it paid the penalty for sin, fully and forever.

—

Take a moment to reflect on the fact that our sins are infinitely offensive to God. Let that fuel your appreciation of the infinite worth of Jesus' sacrifice.

PRAYER POINT

Thank Jesus for being your substitute, for taking your place and receiving the punishment you justly deserve. ✦

PSALM 22:14–18

—

I am poured out like water, and all my bones are disjointed; my heart is like wax, melting within me. My strength is dried up like baked clay; my tongue sticks to the roof of my mouth. You put me into the dust of death. For dogs have surrounded me; a gang of evildoers has closed in on me; they pierced my hands and my feet. I can count all my bones; people look and stare at me. They divided my garments among themselves, and they cast lots for my clothing.

—

———

Though He would be innocent, the Lamb of God would take the punishment for sin upon Himself. God gave His people a picture of how Jesus would die—surrounded by scoffers and unbelievers, exhausted in body and soul. His hands and feet would be pierced as they hung Him up to die, and His killers would disrespect Him so much that they would gamble for His leftover clothes.

What event does this passage describe?

Jesus' death on the cross.

When Jesus died on the cross, was it a quick and easy death?

Parents, discuss with your children that death on a cross is very painful, but that in addition to the pain that He felt in His body, Jesus' death was also difficult because people made fun of Him as He died. Let them know that tomorrow, you'll look at an even more painful part of Jesus' death.

—

When we experience pain and suffering, how does it feel to know that our Savior can empathize with us?

———————————

PRAYER POINT

Take some time to confess to God that it was your sin that put Jesus on the cross. Let that confession lead into gratitude and praise for His willingness to suffer in your place. ✦

ISAIAH 53:5-9

But he was pierced because of our rebellion, crushed because of our iniquities; punishment for our peace was on him, and we are healed by his wounds. We all went astray like sheep; we all have turned to our own way; and the Lord has punished him for the iniquity of us all. He was oppressed and afflicted, yet he did not open his mouth. Like a lamb led to the slaughter and like a sheep silent before her shearers, he did not open his mouth . . . he was struck because of my people's rebellion. He was assigned a grave with the wicked, but he was with a rich man at his death. . . .

Although His people had wandered away from Him, God would do what was necessary to bring them back. He would send His Servant, who would be crushed even though He was perfectly innocent. The Servant would take God's wrath in our place, suffering and dying for our sins; He would do it willingly and without complaint. He would die with the wicked, and He would be buried in the tomb of a rich man.

We saw yesterday in our reading that Jesus' death was painful and humiliating, but can you think of something about His death that was even worse than that?

Sin makes God very angry—the Bible calls this wrath. On the cross, Jesus took God's wrath on Himself even though He didn't deserve it. Receiving the punishment of God's wrath for our sin was worse than any pain imaginable.

This passage says the Servant would be silent like a sheep. If Jesus was innocent, why didn't He speak up to defend Himself?

Jesus knew all along that His mission was to display God's glory by dying in place of sinners like us. He didn't complain about it because He chose to do it in order to save His people.

—

Wrath is often thought of as a character flaw. How is God's wrath consistent with His holy nature?

PRAYER POINT

In light of Jesus' great sacrifice on your behalf, ask God to forgive you for the sin that made it necessary. ✦

PART FIVE

The

PROMISE

of

HIS

RESURRECTION

DECEMBER 19

ISAIAH 53:10–11

—

Yet the LORD was pleased to crush him severely. When you make him a guilt offering, he will see his seed, he will prolong his days, and by his hand, the LORD's pleasure will be accomplished. After his anguish, he will see light and be satisfied. By his knowledge, my righteous servant will justify many, and he will carry their iniquities.

—

—

The Rescuer would be crushed, but that was the plan all along. By His death, God's people would be brought back from their slavery to sin. He would be counted as a sinner and would willingly take the punishment. By faith, God's people would be counted as innocent. But God also planned that the Rescuer's sacrificial death would not be the end of His story—despite His death, God would prolong His days.

Did God plan on letting Jesus stay dead?

No, after Jesus died for our sins, God planned on raising Him back to life, where Jesus would see and be satisfied by what He had done.

What does it mean when it says the Rescuer would "justify" His people? Hint: another translation says He would cause us to be "accounted righteous."

It means that if we have faith in Jesus' sacrifice, God considers us to be without sin. We get the credit for Jesus' perfect life.

Read 2 Corinthians 5:14–15. In light of the death and resurrection of Jesus, how are we to live?

PRAYER POINT

Praise God that His rescue plan always included Jesus' glorious resurrection. ✦

PSALM 16:10

—

For you will not abandon me to Sheol; you will not allow your faithful one to see decay.

—

—

After the Rescuer's death, God would not allow Him to waste away in the grave. The penalty for sin would be complete, and then it would be time for God to declare just how powerful He really is.

Sheol is a word that the Bible sometimes uses to mean *grave* or *tomb*. If Jesus' disciples had remembered this verse, do you think they would have been surprised to find Jesus' tomb empty?

No, they would have realized that an empty tomb is exactly what God had promised.

How does God have the power to bring a dead person back to life?

Because God created all things and has power over life and death.

In what ways are we tempted to take the miracle of the resurrection for granted?

PRAYER POINT

Spend some time meditating on the staggering truth that God has power over life and death. In light of this, ask God to help you grow more confident in Him as you trust His sovereign plan. ✦

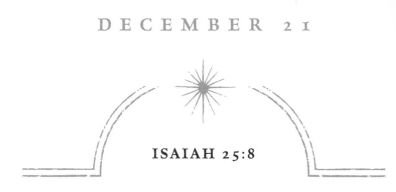

ISAIAH 25:8

—

When he has swallowed up death once and for all, The Lord GOD will wipe away the tears from every face and remove his people's disgrace from the whole earth, for the LORD has spoken.

—

By bringing the Rescuer back from the dead, God would declare victory over sin, Satan, and death. The resurrection would be a promise that all of the miserable effects of our rebellion against God would be swallowed up forever.

Why does this verse point out that God "has spoken"?

Because God is so powerful that when He speaks something, it happens.

The penalty for sin is death. Why was Jesus' resurrection after His death so important?

When God raised Jesus from the dead, it showed that Jesus had truly paid the penalty for sin and that God accepted His sacrifice. God promised that He would raise Jesus up, so it shows that God keeps His promises.

What does it mean to God's people when He says that He will swallow up death forever?

It means that a day is coming when death shall be no more. It also means that those who trust in Jesus will live with Him forever; see John 11:25–26.

—

Read Philippians 3:20–21. How does the reality of Jesus' resurrection impact the way you view the promise of your own future resurrection and glorification?

PRAYER POINT

Reflect on the promise of your future resurrection—of a body and a world made new, free from sin, shame, and sadness. Ask God to hasten the day when He will wipe away every tear. ✦

PART SIX

The

PROMISE

of

HIS

ETERNAL

REIGN

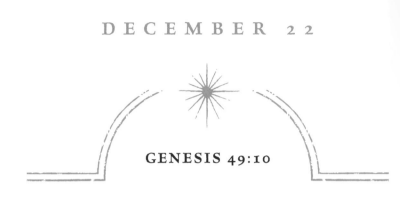

DECEMBER 22

GENESIS 49:10

—

The scepter will not depart from Judah or the staff from between his feet until he whose right it is comes and the obedience of the peoples belongs to him.

—

—

After finishing His great rescue plan, the King from the tribe of Judah would rule over the people of God and they would delight to obey Him. Unlike earthly rulers who eventually lose their power, God said the true King's reign would never end.

From what tribe of Israel did God say the Savior would come?

The tribe of Judah.

From what tribe did Jesus come?

The tribe of Judah. Parents, talk with your children about how this was no coincidence.

A scepter and a staff are things that are held by someone who is in charge. Why is Jesus in charge of all things?

Because all things were created through Him and for Him; see Colossians 1:16.

———

To some people, an eternity of obedience may seem like the opposite of heaven. How does obeying Jesus allow us to experience true freedom?

————————————

PRAYER POINT

Praise Jesus as the King who reigns forever, the King who deserves our joyful obedience. ✦

DECEMBER 23

2 SAMUEL 7:16

—

Your house and kingdom will endure before me forever, and your throne will be established forever.

—

—

God promised King David that his kingdom would go on forever. But David eventually died, and his kingdom wandered away from God. Through the righteous branch from the house of David, God would keep His promise. The Father would display His greatness through the Son by making His kingdom strong forever.

All earthly rulers and kings eventually stop ruling. How long will King Jesus rule?

Forever.

Even if it is supposed to last forever, is there any chance that God's kingdom will be brought to an end?

No, God has said that it will be "established" or "made sure" forever. To be made sure means that it is unshakable.

What is the greatest thing we will get to do in God's eternal kingdom?

We will worship Jesus forever, to the glory of God the Father; see Philippians 2:9–11.

—

Revelation 21:3 says that one day we will dwell with God in His eternal kingdom. How does your life reflect your belief in this future home?

PRAYER POINT

As you live and minister here and now, ask God to give you an eternal, heavenly perspective. ✦

ISAIAH 9:7

—

The dominion will be vast, and its prosperity will never end. He will reign on the throne of David and over his kingdom, to establish and sustain it with justice and righteousness from now on and forever.

—

—

Having saved His people, the Rescuer would rule as the promised King in the line of David. His would be no ordinary kingdom, however. Perfect righteousness, justice, and peace would mark His eternal kingdom.

Why is this kingdom said to have the throne of David?

> *To remind us that God had promised that the Savior King would come from King David's family.*

What kind of kingdom has God built?

> *It is peaceful, just, and holy. It will last forever.*

In the end, what will Jesus do in the kingdom?

> *He will rule alongside His Father, magnifying Him by giving Him the supreme position in the kingdom; see 1 Corinthians 15:24.*

——

Waiting is difficult; meditate on how living in anticipation of the perfect kingdom can actually give you joy right now.

———————————————

PRAYER POINT

Praise God that, one day, sin and injustice will be no more. Ask Him to help you reflect that future reality in the way you live today. ✦

DANIEL 7:14

He was given dominion and glory and a kingdom, so that those of every people, nation, and language should serve him. His dominion is an everlasting dominion that will not pass away, and his kingdom is one that will not be destroyed.

The Rescuer, the great Savior who would free His people from sin and bring them back to God, would take His rightful place with His Father as the everlasting King. His kingdom would include people from every part of the world, and all of His people would love Him endlessly, giving God the glory that He deserves.

Who will be included in God's kingdom?

People from every people group and nation. Most will not look like us or talk like us, but God will be glorified by saving so many different kinds of people.

What does it mean to have dominion?

It means to have authority, to be the boss.

Who deserves to be the boss of all things now and forever?

Only God. He alone is worthy of receiving praise and glory from all people for all time.

—

How are you bringing the news of God's eternal kingdom to all peoples, nations, and languages?

PRAYER POINT

Praise God and give Him the glory He deserves. Thank Him for fulfilling the rescue plan He promised to us long ago. ✦

Now spend some time this Christmas Day celebrating God's faithfulness in sending us the long-expected Savior. Read the epilogue, *Promises Kept*, to learn how the promises of God that we have explored this month have come true in Jesus, the Expected One.

EPILOGUE:
PROMISES KEPT

—

Many years after these promises were made, Jesus was born in Bethlehem. He was born into the family line of King David, but His birth was a miracle because God Himself, through the Holy Spirit, brought it about. A man named John the Baptist announced the arrival of Jesus and pointed to Him as the One who would rescue our rebellious world from sin. Jesus lived His entire life in perfect obedience to God the Father, showing that He was the promised Immanuel—God in our midst. The precious Son of God humbled Himself on our behalf as He walked the earth, calling people to turn away from sin and follow Him.

Most people did not believe this lowly man could be the long-awaited King, so they dismissed Jesus as a liar. Although He was perfectly innocent, Jesus laid down His life willingly as His accusers put Him to death. They pierced His hands and feet as they nailed Him to a wooden cross. But God intended this evil act for a greater purpose: by His death, Jesus became an atoning sacrifice—the true Passover Lamb—taking sin's penalty for all who trust in Him. Not only did He take our punishment on Himself, He also gave us the credit for His perfect obedience, making a way for us to be brought back into God's family. God was so pleased with Jesus' perfect sacrifice that He raised Him from the dead and exalted Him to His heavenly throne, where He reigns forever to the glory of God the Father.

Jesus, the long-expected mighty Rescuer, has crushed Satan and now welcomes into His kingdom all those who abandon sin and trust in Him completely. Are you trusting in Him?

One day, Jesus will return to make all things new, to do away with sin and sadness forever. He has promised this and, as we have seen, He is God and He keeps His promises. Are you expecting Him?

ADVENT FAMILY MEMORIES

ADVENT FAMILY MEMORIES

ADVENT FAMILY MEMORIES

ADVENT FAMILY MEMORIES

ADVENT FAMILY MEMORIES

ADVENT FAMILY MEMORIES

ADVENT FAMILY MEMORIES

ADVENT FAMILY MEMORIES

ADVENT FAMILY MEMORIES

ALSO AVAILABLE
— *from* —
SCOTT JAMES

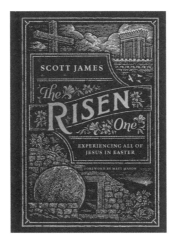

The Risen One
Pairing with *The Expected One* or used by itself, *The Risen One* is a short and sweet devotional with 12 weekly readings, helping families everywhe observe Lent and experience all Jesus is for us in the Easter season.

Use along with *The Expected One* to walk from Advent to Easter, rightly focusing your heart on the One we both anticipate and worship.

Where is Wisdom?
This visual tour through the poetry of Job 28 leads young readers on a treasure hunt through the wonders of God's creation, all in search of tru wisdom that comes from God alone.